CW00503963

Motivational Interviewing

Promote Confidence and Esteem with Dialectical Behavioral Therapy to Understanding Borderline Personality, Bipolar Disorder, Self-Acceptance and Commitment (Quotes Included)

Wendy Robbins

ABOUT THE AUTHOR

Wendy Robbins is a school psychology professor at one of the best schools in Missouri. She was one of the first experts to approach Classroom Check-up, an assessment-based teacher consultation model. Her research focuses on preventing disruptive behavior problems in children and increasing school's implementation of evidence-based practices.

To have a greater impact on people she decided to write her amazing 7 book series called "The Happiness Education Factory".

Wendy Robbins wishes everyone good progress!

© **Copyright 2020 by Wendy Robbins All rights reserved.**

This document is geared towards providing exact and reliable information in regards to the topic and issue covered. The publication is sold with the idea that the publisher is not required to render accounting, officially permitted, or otherwise, qualified services. If advice is necessary, legal or professional, a practiced individual in the profession should be ordered.

- From a Declaration of Principles which was accepted and approved equally by a Committee of the American Bar

Association and a Committee of Publishers and Associations.

In no way is it legal to reproduce, duplicate, or transmit any part of this document in either electronic means or in printed format. Recording of this publication is strictly prohibited and any storage of this document is not allowed unless with written permission from the publisher. All rights reserved.

The information provided herein is stated to be truthful and consistent, in that any liability, in terms of inattention or otherwise, by any usage or abuse of any policies, processes, or directions contained within is the solitary and utter responsibility of the recipient reader. Under no circumstances will any legal responsibility or blame be held against the publisher for any reparation, damages, or monetary loss due to the information herein, either directly or indirectly.

Respective authors own all copyrights not held by the publisher.

The information herein is offered for informational purposes solely, and is universal as so. The presentation of the information is without contract or any type of guarantee assurance.

The trademarks that are used are without any consent, and the publication of the trademark is without permission or backing by the trademark owner. All trademarks and brands within this book are for clarifying purposes only and are the owned by the owners themselves, not affiliated with this document.

Table of contents

Introduction

Motivational interviewing is a method of therapy designed to help people overcome their contrasting ambivalent and contradictory emotions and insecurities. Everything to help them get the inspiration they need so that they can feel more motivated to alter entire or even portions of the behavior. A motivational interview is a short-term method, both realistic and empathetic. Through this form of therapy, the fact that life-changing choices are complex and daunting for everyone is part of the process. Motivational coaching has been developed with addiction or dependency in mind, but the guidelines extend to several emotional and physical health problems such as:

- Anxiety.

- Depression.

- Gambling problems.

- Prescription/Illicit drug abuse.

- Pornography addictions.

For the potential to be incorporated in combination with certain forms of counseling, persuasive interviewing stands out from certain schools of thinking. Used in conjunction with treatments such as CBT, REBT, and other strategies, this may enhance therapy effectiveness. People searching for supportive coaching resources should often utilize drug reduction and 12-step programs to assist in their recovery.

Findings suggest that positive interview elements help people stay interested in recovery and create commitment. It is important to many in recovery, particularly for those needing drug misuse care.

Since motivational interviewing was designed for diversion, the methods have resulted in positive outcomes. Individuals are gradually shifting away from addiction's ambivalence and toward a transition in treatment.

An interviewer's role is largely in keeping an open conversation, listening carefully, and reflecting back all the customer's thoughts said, for a client to hear all those reasons again and the motivations, but this time he said otherwise. This counseling is short-term and may be between 1-3 sessions, but it may also become part of long-term therapy. There are two aims of the Motivational Interview. The first is to find a way to improve motivation; the second focuses on participating. MOTIVATIONAL INTERVIEW is designed to help consumers communicate and appreciate their needs; it lets them gain inspiration, clarity, and a way to connect with the transition. It is possible to combine this type of counseling with certain support groups, cognitive therapy, or even other kinds of intervention.

The main goal of the Motivational Interview is to encourage positive thoughts in the patient and make them look at life in a different way!

Chapter 1. What is Motivational Interviewing?

Motivational interview is a psychotherapeutic technique that aims to push a person away from a state of indecision or confusion and to gain inspiration to make good choices and accomplish defined objectives. William R. Miller and Stephen Rollnick founded Motivational Interviewing thirty years ago as a means to get beyond the problem of poor desire to improve.

Motivation is essential to progress in treating addiction, while lack of motivation can serve as a major obstacle.

The prevailing thought in the early 1980s was that lack of motivation needs to be discussed through confrontation in therapy. In this method, the psychiatrist will outline the causes for the desire for improvement, state the negative factors correlated with lack of progress, and push the client to improve as a means of encouragement. Motivational Interviewing isn't a new idea. This was developed in the early 1980s when American physician William R. Miller, Md, introduced a clinical method for individuals with drug disorders that he had utilized with considerable results. In the contemporary era, Miller and his colleagues define motivational interviewing as *"a directive, client-centered counseling style for eliciting behavior change by helping clients to explore and resolve ambivalence."*

Essentially, it's a way of shifting a conversation 's course to encourage the patient's willingness to improve and giving him or her the courage to do so. Unlike many other evolving approaches used by health care practitioners (such as methods of awareness, coercion, and fear), motivational interviews are more concentrated, goal-oriented, and patient-centered. A key idea is that the inspiration for improvement will come from the individual, rather than from the practitioner.

While the majority of the research and study motivational interviewing requires intensive counseling, there is proof that very short (five-minute) sessions have beneficial effects, particularly where patients become extremely resistant to change. Motivational questioning is also a technique of tremendous potential for time-pressed family doctors and representatives of their treatment team. Motivational interviewing by Miller and Rollnick differs in that it uses a polite and respectful, cooperative process between the client and the therapist to spark motivation and make change happen.

Instead of behaving in a hostile or confrontational fashion, the psychiatrist works with the client to discuss his emotions, particularly ambivalence regarding transition, and help the person discover their own motives. The therapist will become a support person, allowing patients to make the right choices and start coming to their own judgments without having to feel outside tension to do so. Conducting an interview shares similarity with person-centered (humanistic) therapy.

Throughout the 1950s and 1960s Carl Rogers developed this therapeutic philosophy and method of counseling as an antidote to psychoanalytical and behaviorist ideas. Person-centered thinking is based on the idea that people in them possess innate goodness and value. It is the therapist's work to allow the clients to create their own best version.

1.1 Key Aspects of Motivational Interviewing

The phrase "the spirit of motivational interviewing" is commonly used in discussions regarding motivational interviewing to refer to how this technique is developed, as opposed to the basic techniques that are used. The "spirit" consists of three constituents. They are:

Collaboration. The psychiatrist should try to approach the problem from the person's point of view, instead of becoming argumentative or confrontational toward the individual. The psychiatrist is not the specialist in these terms, as no one has a greater view of the person's situation than the individual. The goal here is to serve as a tool rather than a persuader for the therapist.

Evocation. For certain types of treatment, such as cognitive-behavioral counseling, the consultant provides the person with the knowledge as an opportunity to alter their way of thought, attitudes, or behaviors. This strategy will at times cause feelings of defensiveness. Motivational interviewing has the objective of creating a client's internal commitment to change. The psychiatrist listens rather than speaks and points out the customer's own experiences rather than forcing expectations. This means the client would be more involved in holding the shift running for a longer time.

Autonomy. Motivational coaching places all the focus on the client. The psychiatrist displays an appreciation for the duty of the individual, and the capacity to make choices.

1.2 Principles of Motivational Interviewing

The elements above act as an overarching understanding of positive questioning views. The therapist is entrusted inside the sessions with certain concepts and initiatives that are used to make the time more advantageous and profitable. A therapist will:

Empathize with the Patient. It is one of the core principles of person-centered therapy which includes motivational interviewing. The therapist's role here is to develop an awareness of the client's problems, challenges, and development obstacles. By doing this, with correct transparency, the customer is more accessible and freer, because there is a shortage of judgment and critique. One therapist might tell, "I can fully realize why drug use in this situation seems appealing."

Develop discrepancy. It becomes the therapist's job, with the second principle, to have the patient point out the difference between what they are actually doing and what their goals are. If the aim is to be happier and have a good life, it might get in the way of using heroin every day. The psychiatrist should of course utilize nonconfrontationally oriented approaches to achieve this. Only a series of questions are asked by the therapist to lead the patient to this logical conclusion.

Resistance is Important. Motivational interviewing assumes that during this phase there may be some reluctance and reticence from the customer. Holding the non-confrontational beliefs in place, the educator does not try to push or pressure the individual into approval. The psychiatrist should seek to recognize the client's point of view to suppress the temptation to fix what may be perceived as faulty ways of thinking when giving the person different forms of thinking.

Support the Belief in improvement/self-efficacy. Most clients have struggled to sustain their sobriety with little results, particularly those struggling with addictions, rehab, and relapse. That can make them less hopeful for future success. The consultant should focus on highlighting aspects of success and documenting a list of occasions where the person has been willing to reach their target.

The preceding sections explored the aims of positive interviewing as a therapy method, and the values a psychiatrist strives to fulfill through care. This segment addresses what should be used in a standard motivational interview session.

Open-ended queries hold significance. Several queries have a straightforward answer based on a number or a "yes or no." Open-ended queries are special in that they need more duration and information. Therapists using constructive interviews will use certain prompts to involve the client in a conversation that allows the client to become fully conscious of their emotions, feelings, and values. Open-ended queries allow the individual patient leverage while the practitioner pursues their guide.

Affirmations. An affirmation is a therapist's assertion in support of a client's decision or behavior. The affirmation will be adequate and valid if properly done. The psychiatrist should not explicitly praise the harmful habits simply to improve the client's trust. Such therapist comments are important in developing the customer's sense of control and confidence in his desire to improve.

Reflections. In motivational interviewing, insightful listening is as critical as in many forms of counseling, including individual-centered, Dialectical Behavior Counseling, and CBT. A reflection involves being listened to by the therapist and reflecting on the information. It is not simply a restatement of what the patient says. It is a way to reassure the psychiatrist that he respects the perspective of the person. It establishes the connection and greatly reduces ambivalence.

Summaries are important after every session. For the untrained mind, summaries and observations sound the same. Summaries vary in that they review knowledge to reveal specific problems and themes. Summaries, however, can help to move towards transformation by highlighting client differences and discrepancies.

Change talk by the Patient. If the four previous aspects of the session perform well, there will be a shift in chat. This act is performed by the individual instead of the psychiatrist. The client will make explicit comments on these improvements and their benefits. Talks on transition are split into two groups. The first is tentative, and it covers the motivation for improvement, appreciation of their potential to improve, the justification for improvement, and the necessity for improvement. Preparatory talk about change is an encouraging sign that change and true progress is on the surface. The second form of change-talk is much more encouraging: execution. This requires declarations of dedication to progress, triggering readiness and preparedness, and implementing action to bring in improvement.

1.3 When is Motivational Interviewing Needed?

This type of counseling is mostly used when there arises a need to resolve problems with addiction or when a person simply wants to learn how to manage certain life-changing conditions that might affect their health, such as heart problems, asthma, or diabetes. This is a form of intervention that aims to help people find and maintain their motivation in order to change one's behavior that prevents their process of healing and improving.

MOTIVATIONAL INTERVIEW is also used to support individuals mentally and help them socially lead healthy lives, and also to train them for more therapy. The goal is to help people feel empowered to remain prepared for the transition that faces them, so they need to make adjustments. It's also beneficial to the citizens who still feel negative or upset. Committing to a transition is not the only aspect of the equation because this therapy will often rely on encouraging patients to find the correct strength and work through various phases of their emotions.

Motivational workshops are also used to discuss obesity and the treatment of problems in poor wellbeing such as diabetes, lung failure, and asthma. This intervention helps motivate people to change their behaviors which prevents them from making healthy lifestyle choices. It also can prepare people for additional, extra specific types of treatments. Research has also shown that this intervention will work well with people starting unmotivated or unprepared for change.

To those who are not inspired to improve it becomes less beneficial. Motivational questioning often helps frustrated or aggressive individuals. They may not be prepared to commit to keep changing but motivational interviewing may help them move through the interpersonal stages of change needed to find the motivation that they need.

A positive trainer will allow people to address their desire for improvement and their own motivations for having to improve, in a friendly manner. The interviewer's job is primarily to elicit a conversation about transition and engagement. The investigator reacts to the client's feelings and expresses them so that the client can hear their motives and intentions reflected back to them. Motivational interviewing is typically short-term therapy that requires only 1 to 2 sessions, although it can also be included with other long-term therapies as an intervention.

Motivational interviewing emerged from a person-centered, or client-centered approach to mediation and treatment created by Carl Roger as a way to help individuals succeed in the painful phase of transition. The cycle is double-edged. The first aim is to increase the enthusiasm of the individual and the second is for the participant to pursue the effort to improve. Rather than merely expressing a need or willingness to alter, having themselves convey an out loud dedication has been found to greatly enhance the motivation of a person to eventually implement such improvements. The therapist's role lies more in trying to listen than in getting involved. Often, motivational interviews are combined or immediately followed with other interventions, such as cognitive therapy, support groups like stress management training, and Alcoholics Anonymous. Search for an empathetic and supportive mental health worker and a strong listener. Seeking an interviewer with both advanced qualifications and expertise, because persuasive interviewing is an ability that develops over the practice. Look for a positive interviewer with whom you feel confident collaborating, in addition to seeking someone with the correct educational history and applicable experience.

Chapter 2. How to Motivational Interview?

Motivational interviewing is a short suggestion method that may be beneficial in helping people resolve resistance to create lifestyle improvements, such as weight reduction or smoking cessation. The physician's aim is not to fix the patient's dilemma, but to help the patient overcome her or his ambivalence, gain some motivation, and think the improvement in behavior is feasible. Motivational interviewing ends with a warm, constructive partnership between doctor and patient. It allows the doctor to show empathy for the patient and to understand that the aversion of a patient to improvement is usually evoked by situational circumstances rather than a moral defect or the urge to make it more complicated for the person. In other words, when a patient struggles to change the doctor should not take it personally. Rather, the practitioner ought to "let go" of the result, encourage self-efficacy, enable the patient to be accountable for their own success, and allow the patient to define and express their fundamental beliefs and priorities.

For instance, if an obese patient establishes a physical exercise target of merely "going to the mailbox every day," the doctor will demonstrate appreciation for that aim, even if it may sound low. The goal should not be to solve the problem of the client or even to form a strategy; the purpose is to help the patient fix his or her indifference, establish some strength, and truly think that change in behavior is achievable. Most physicians are rapid to propose a solution because of time limitations and medical knowledge; however, doing this often denies the client the chance to evaluate various courses of action as well as the associated costs and benefits. Those courses of action are often confusing, contradictory, and profoundly personal. Allowing the individual to discuss these problems improves the likelihood of achieving suitable treatment for the condition. The "OARS" acronym describes the four essential elements of motivational interviewing.

1. Open-ended queries. Avoid asking such questions that can easily be answered with a "yes" or a "no." Broad questions enable patients to respond with maximum freedom without fear of a correct or wrong answer. It can be as simple as, "What's happened to you since we met last time? Another query, perfect for almost all, would be, "If you had one thing you needed to alter to better your health, what would it be?"

2. Affirmations. Never underestimate the ability to express empathy in tough spots or celebrate the achievements of patients. Take pride in their performance as you study the priorities of patients, and express your happiness. One of the writers (CF) also offers gold stars to patients-the the exact ones that are awarded in primary school. Patients love to get them and proudly wear them.

3. Reflective listening. Patients always get the answers; the job of the practitioner is to help direct them. Reflective listening means encouraging people to share their feelings and then, instead of asking them what to do, understanding the meaning of what they have expressed, to stimulate dialogue and enable them to come up with a concept for improvement.

Here's one example:

Patient: "I wish I didn't consume fast food too much."

Doctor: "You eat fast food on a daily basis."

Patient: "Every day, pretty much. I know I'm not supposed to, but that's easier.'

Doctor: "It's easier as you don't have to plan meals and cook them."

Patient: "So I can pass the drive-through just through."

Doctor: "So you wouldn't want to give up fast food convenience but you want to eat healthier."

Patient: "Hmm. ... I think a few balanced things are on the table."

This is therefore important to consider the attitude of the individual on what he or she is asking you. For instance, "You said that because of your weight, you are not going to go in public in a bathing suit. That seems to make summertime very stressful for you." Reflecting the declarations and feelings of patients back to them perpetuates self-efficacy, and enables the conversation to continue to move forward.

4. Summaries. Summarizing means recapturing what has been stated by the participant, drawing attention to the main aspects of the conversation, and encouraging the participant to fix any misunderstandings and incorporating something lacking. Summaries may take place during the visit but are especially useful when getting the visit to an end. Often it is helpful to conclude a review with an accessible declaration such as "I wonder what you feel at this stage" or "I wonder what you think your next move will be."

Through these strategies, you will help establish a common and realistic target for the individual. The individual will believe that he or she is really trying to reach the target, not just seek. Ask the patient to clarify the target (this helps ensure agreement), and afterward write it in the report, allowing the patient to know that you can discuss it together during the next appointment, or maybe via phone or maybe e-mail between the visits.

2.1 Do's and Don'ts of Motivational Interviewing

Motivational interviewing is a series of communication strategies that can cause improvements in behavior in people with chronic conditions including diabetes. For some providers, that communication style can become a dramatic shift. Think this way of MOTIVATIONAL INTERVIEW: The provider usually steers the vessel, tends to bring the fuel, as well as charts the course. The counselor is clearly the rudder, acting as a compass, and the participant steers in the Motivational Interviewing. Ken Resnicow, Ph.D., provides Positive INTERVIEW-style excerpts and illustrations below.

DO: Listen to your patient's fears and problems carefully.

The first approach of Motivational Interview form is to respond to the patient's anxieties and issues. We term that "playing with opposition." When someone issues with their medicine or adjustments of behavior, the first thing we need to do is react to what the problem is and seek not to pressure, suggest or resolve it.

Just listen, and reflect back for the first few minutes. Reflecting back, for example, could be something like: "It's difficult for you just because your husband still likes candy and does not like veggies." Or, "It's difficult because your children haven't introduced them to these things." Or, "It's difficult because it requires more." The first step of energizing the patient is looking back on the patient's problems.

DO: Pause before you discuss how your patient can bring changes in his life.

In MOTIVATIONAL INTERVIEW format, we are taking a little longer to get to the process of "how" and invest more time in the process of "thought". Many clinicians are somewhat over-anxious to move to the "how" level, which includes issues such as preparing for practice, establishing targets, and looking at different diets and medications for exercise. In Motivational Interview, we postpone the process and advise providers to focus two-thirds of the time mostly on "why" or only one-third mostly on "how." Providers can be disoriented, so there is a sense that it may take longer. In reality, over time it's probably more efficient. It is a reallocation of the time of a provider, within this more time is spent paying attention to and trying to respond to the barriers and worries of the patient. Often, that is the essence of comfort.

DO: Listen to a patient's ideas and insights.

The next step, after reflecting on the problems and feelings of a patient, is what we call the talk about "making improvement." It's a sequence of having the individual express how good a change in behavior would be for him or her, and reasonable ways of acting. So, a provider would perhaps say, "What are your concepts on how you can make this situation better?" And then the doctor would listen to the patient's confidence carefully.

The patient might say, along with the hardships and obstacles, "I like to walk," or "There's the latest gym." A highly qualified provider may pick up the trail's aroma because sufferers often refer to what they're willing to do so in an oblique manner. During the talk patients sometimes lose crumbs on what they're able to do.

DO: Collaborate.

When an individual has a high desire and starts to explore strategies to create improvements in behavior, a practitioner may function together — respectfully. You'll want to discuss how well the patient's ready and worthy of making improvements at the moment.

We would probably start in the MOTIVATIONAL INTERVIEW style with a rather small step by simply stating, "So, you prefer walking?" Let that sit down; let that individual explain his thoughts and feelings.

Then perhaps we can say, "How are you seeing walking fit into your life, if at all?

"So, with any form of prescription, we are pretty careful. Now, if the person volunteers — "I'm going to walk with my dog twice a week" — we 'd reinforce absolutely.

DON'T: Fix, pressure, or control.

Motivational Interviewing invigorates patients, in step with their physicians and backers, to take a lead in managing their health. We are telling providers to be wary of forced remedies or dialect control. Doctors have these brilliant theories because they want the individual to solve them, but we notice drugs do not seem to solve them.

"You have to, you can, you really should, it's easier, it's necessary, do it for me," are the key leading terms of therapy and we place them together under the context of incentive control — which can be dangerous, rendering the individual aggressive or shut down.

We're trying to avoid language controlling because it elicits resistance. The research is very explicit on individuals who do things when they were made to feel bad, ashamed, or coerced by someone. The long-term prognosis for improvements in the behavior of these persons is low.

Do not use scare tactics.

Instead by utilizing "fear, evidence, and input," as we suggest, we seek to energize the behavior improvement with certain items in the person's life that are of high importance that have a ton of salience. We usually don't want to get people excited by scaring them.

In the short term, individuals are generally able to make adjustments when they are terrified — as they get infected first — but it fades away after a fairly short amount of time, so the problem is how to maintain the individual energized after the initial panic has worn off.

Do not Neglect to appreciate the patient's efforts.

This may be challenging to self-manage diabetes, including gaining weight or altering lifetime dietary patterns. Figure out a way to admire the patient and acknowledge his/her efforts, even if no or little success is achieved. If someone's A1C hasn't moved but they've been taking their metformin or exercising three times a week, say, "you've put so much effort into this." React to the anger, dissatisfaction, and terror of your patient. It won't solve the immediate problem, but it will make the individual realize their work hasn't been wasted. As compared to only "fixing it" and thinking, "Okay, we're going to find a different drug," it makes the patient feel understood. With time, the intuition will help keep your patient-focused and contribute to improved outcomes.

2.2 Processes of Motivational Interview

Motivational interviewing is not really a psychotherapeutic treatment but instead a method to be utilized in combination with other systematic therapy strategies "for encouraging improvement in patients who would either feel indifferent or perhaps unwilling to improve their circumstances. Motivational Interviewing consists of 4 main, client-centered systems that function together in order to help the person identify and progress toward his/her goals. These processes are working together to provide guidance for the patients to motivate themselves to adapt and move forward appropriately. Motivational interviewing focuses on helping the person realize his / her own personal and genuine inspiration for altering behavioral problems by steering communication with the patient in a certain way. While the clinician often directs the practice in a particular way, positive coaching will strive and motivate the participant and develop and devise a roadmap for pushing him or herself towards suitable clinical objectives.

Engaging

Developing a clear psychological connection is a critical element of motivational interviewing. Specific qualities such as empathy, tolerance, and emphasis on consumer needs and shared interests shape the foundations for such compliance. Mutual consideration is made feasible in this part by maintaining a level of partnership between psychologist and consumer, such that power politics will not stymy the patient-centered method. Encouraging a spirit of fair cooperation in a therapeutic arrangement requires the client to be able to consider not only the talents, experience, expertise, and beliefs of the individual in the research cycle but also to rely on them.

Engaging also comprises four patient-centered skills, shortened with the OARS acronym. OARS include interviewing open questions, asserting the strengths of clients, reflecting on whatever they might wish to convey, but they have not spoken about it out loud, and summing up what has happened in any therapeutic contact.

Focusing

Whereas some psychological environments will arrive with some clear main points or aims – as many will not, for example, in any case of court-ordered therapy. Many clients may come to you with content they are eager to get to put the effort in instantly, and some will seek input and guidance on the further steps to be taken. Focusing is to help the client decide what really matters to him/her and use that knowledge to prepare the stage for the job. The therapist and the client can, of course, decide on the targets, but Motivational Interviewing focuses on helping the client to strive and define his/her own field of stuckness, uneasiness or challenge and establish goals accordingly.

Evoking

When a goal is established and unanimously decided, evoking includes identifying the emotional desire of the individual and the incentive to improve. One important part of the evoking process is about being capable of recognizing when clients talk about something that suggests they might be willing or willing to move towards change. Patients should create a declaration that reflects a need for progress, that they hope they should improve, that they think about repercussions if they don't progress, or that improvement is completely vital to a willingness to go on. These declarations provide crucial details on whether the customer is available, eager, or able to adjust or not. But if you know how to invite the "change talk" of this sort then it is a significant part of the interview. Open-ended queries are a helpful way to elicit this kind of conversation to help appreciate the interaction to desire to improve that the individual has against. Another useful approach to collect knowledge is by encouraging clients to offer suggestions or explanations on their answers to your open-ended queries regarding the transition. As mentioned in the OARS acronym, be certain to assess and also summarize once the person engages in the talk about change.

Planning

Through motivational coaching, the crucial part about the preparation phase is that its strategy emerges from the participants and is focused on their own beliefs, experience, and self-awareness. All of the 4 phases are oriented towards promoting and developing the desire of the clients to improve, and any efforts to "take the reins" throughout the preparation phase on behalf of the psychologist that disrupt or just reverse the sense of confidence of the client. That said, you are entirely responsible, as a counselor, for including your expertise at the time its justified. For example, consumers can communicate plainly that they wish to improve, have to improve, or even are able to change, although they might be confused about how they are supposed to do that. That is where the know-how falls in. So long so your guidance is received, your feedback will be a vital aspect of leading the consumer into making a strategy they feel better about and encouraged to adhere to. If you are not sure if your guidance is being sought or not, you also can always just ask.

Chapter 3. Overcome Crisis and Trauma with Auto-Counseling

Auto-Therapy is reshaping the provision of qualified counseling. Formal therapy sessions may trigger high anxiety rates and sound unnerving because of the office-like environment. You can now receive therapeutic counseling with Auto Therapy while driving around the town, or to a particular destination, and back. The groundbreaking modern therapy methodology allows the use of neuroscience, vehicles, and interaction interrelationships to create a special and valuable encounter. From walking to a local park to traveling by a childhood home to remembering a significant incident in life; my job is to offer a supportive and innovative therapy experience. Stay ready as we travel at a rate of counseling while experiencing regular landscape change. Perfect for those clients who feel repressed by meeting in a central location with the therapist. Tends to make mental health care more available to a larger human demographic. Via mutual interactions on the path, you and your doctor connect while creating a solution for your mental health issues.

The informal setup about being in a moving car leaves you feeling less nervous and comfortable to share your thoughts and feelings. All the clinicians attached to that vehicle are professionally trained as psychotherapists and drivers. Every driver has to pass a defensive driving course, a driver's test carried out by the professional staff, have insurance coverage, and have CPR certification. The hospitals guarantee to have their drivers certified. Cameras are mounted within the cars to ensure protection. All captured video shall stay private and unnoticed until there is a lack of health. Your security and confidentiality are paramount.

For starters, it is best to arrange a meeting to fully understand the wholly unique and suited therapy approach. There will be tackling other real-life conditions and mental health problems. Working with your therapist, you'll both determine if Auto Therapy fits your needs best.

If you are not happy, you may cancel your Auto Therapy appointments at any moment, in order to continue with conventional counseling. Try to do that 24 hours before your meeting is scheduled and everything will be done to fit your needs.

The reaction to a traumatic incident differs greatly among individuals, but certain simple, typical symptoms also occur.

Emotional signs include:

- anger

- sadness

- fear

- denial

- shame

These might lead to:

- insomnia

- nightmares

- emotional outbursts

- difficulty with relationships

Physical symptoms found commonly:

- dizziness

- nausea

- altered sleep patterns

- headaches

- changes in appetite

- gastrointestinal problems

Psychological disorders might include:

- depression

- PTSD

- dissociative disorders

- anxiety

- substance abuse problems

The longer you exist, the more likely it would be for us to suffer a trauma. A trauma is the reaction to a distressing or traumatic occurrence that overwhelms the capacity of a person to deal with it, triggers emotions of helplessness, weakens the sense of identity, and one's capacity to sense the full spectrum of experiences and emotions.

It doesn't allow discrimination and is widespread worldwide. A *World Mental Health* research published by *World Health Organization* discovered that trauma had occurred to at least *one-third out of more than 125,000 individuals surveyed in twenty-six countries*. That percentage grew to 70% as the category became confined to individuals with core conditions as described by *DSM-IV* (a description used in the *Mental Disorders Diagnostic and Statistical Manual, 4th Edition*). Yet such figures are only for recorded instances; the real figure is much bigger.

Safety is important! When the stressful condition continues, get some support in keeping yourself safe and healthy. You might need some support for locating a safe place to live. Speak to someone who you know about whatever happened. It can even be good to talk with family and friends. Understanding and support can be of great help in a difficult time. You wouldn't have to face that on your own. Know that to someone who has been through a stressful experience, how you feel is very natural. Give yourself all the time that you need. Know that the way you feel does not continue, and you'll be able to move on with life by coping with the worries and emotions. Be patient with yourself. Understand that the transition will take a bit of time. Spend some time doing fun stuff-resting, cycling, enjoying lovely locations, having mates. Plan on doing nice things every day.

Confronting circumstances related to the stressful experience would be necessary ... but do so slowly. You may want to go back into the workforce, but at least go for only a few hours and then build it up gradually. Don't deal with narcotics and alcohol. They are just going to make it worse.

Try to come up with other ways to relax. Although there are zero clear standards for determining which incidents may trigger signs of post-trauma, situations usually include lack of authority, deception, misuse of influence, impotence, discomfort, frustration, and/or deprivation.

The event does not need to arise to the level of a war or a natural disaster, or an assault personally to profoundly affect a person and change their experiences. The traumatic circumstances that trigger symptoms of post-trauma differ and vary significantly from individual to individual. It is indeed very contextual and it is crucial to keep in your mind that its reaction is defined much more than the trigger.

3.1 How to Cope with Traumatic Symptoms

Always make sure that you're around with people. Do not go back home to an empty house. You can always ask a relative or a friend to stay with you. Talk to others about the incident. Talking lets you work past the responses. Remember the event is now over, and that you are safe now. Have some physical exercise where possible. That will help to burn off most of your stress and depression. Avoid the use of medication, sedatives, or sleeping tablets (they would just intensify the sensation and not encourage you to control your feelings).

Restrict the intake of stimulants (coffee, tea, candy, cola, or cigarettes) if you don't want the body to get any more irritated than it is now. Consider consuming it, particularly though you don't feel like doing it. When you are not able to relax, do not lay in bed, twist, and switch-get up and do something before you are exhausted. Know that the responses are a natural trauma outcome, which should pass in time. Seek to re-enter the daily schedule as quickly as possible. You may need to slowly introduce yourself to seemingly difficult tasks. If you're feeling uncomfortable, afraid, or anxious, take a few long, slow breaths and remember you 're safe and now the trauma is over. Please ensure you do something to relax and enjoyable things and be kind to yourself. Keep sharing the experience with relatives, acquaintances, and coworkers. This will help you get over your emotions. Even if you feel a bit distant from others, don't dismiss their support. Don't worry about emotions. Keep sharing the experience with relatives, acquaintances, and coworkers. This will assist you to move past your emotions. Even if you feel a bit distant from others, don't dismiss their support. Don't care about emotions. Work on your overall levels of stress by ensuring you have adequate sleep, a good diet, and regular workouts. Practice relaxation in helping to lower nervous tension. Drive carefully around the home, and be more careful with machinery. Fatalities after severe stress become more common. Let yourself have time to deal with the memories. Also, you need patience and commitment. There could be some aspects of the encounter that will be hard to forget. If your reaction is still seriously disrupting your life, please speak with your doctor. Start the conversation with your local doctor. One other option is to contact a mental health center in your local community and to talk to a professional. If you've been sexually assaulted, many cities and towns will be able to provide you with a sexual abuse or rape crisis center. Your local phone book is supposed to help you find your nearest center.

Unless the pain is war-related, the best way to get treatment might be for Veteran Affairs in the region. A number of colleges provide anxiety care by their department of counseling or psychiatry. For counselors and therapists, specialist organizations may be willing to help you receive the treatment you need. One thing common to humans is the experience of grief after a loss. The most severe grief typically follows a loved person's death, maybe because death is so final and humans feel a strong sense of loss. Although the discussion would primarily concentrate on bereavement, common responses exist with several various forms of death, e.g. breakup of a friendship, pet death, a career, a lifestyle, a leg. The strong emotions experienced after a loss are really a normal, healthy part of the journey of healing, and eventually result in learning to live with the loss. However, certain problems in working through the cycle may contribute to depression.

Any medications may be effective in managing PTSD. Studies reported contradictory outcomes. Antidepressant medications have demonstrated improvement. Benzodiazepines like Valium can offer some immediate relief from the symptoms, but they are addictive so you may ultimately require bigger doses to achieve the same benefit. They're not approved for usage in the long run. The treatment itself cannot be as beneficial for you as having conjoint treatment (CBT).

Strategies may be used to reduce the degree of anticipation, if too strong. Hopefully, this can increase your sense of security and health, and help you deal with traumatic memories and causes involved with the trauma. A few important tips:

Get daily sleep, and follow a well-balanced diet of frequent meals. Do something every single day to relax. Find a comfortable place to relax. Clear your eyes. Practice the one-minute slow respiration method. And relax your muscles. Feel the feeling of relief. For at least eight weeks, practice once maybe twice daily. Reduce consumption of stimulants, such as nicotine and coffee. Do not use alcohol or some other medications to assist with coping. They will make matters worse. Plan on doing nice things every day. Get back to your daily routine-usual work, meals, etc. Learn to regulate your breathing by following certain instructions to rising anxiety symptoms. Hold your breath for 6 seconds and time it. Inhale and exhale every 6 seconds. Say 'relax' whilst breathing out. Stop for a minute or when you lose your fear. Practice four times a day; one-minute slow breathing then it'll be easy to use it when you want it. Gradually, it's necessary to confront the circumstances and memories, you may have prevented. It is important to pursue the assistance of a professionally qualified therapist in delivering cognitive behavioral PTSD therapy and continue and overcome the fears. Exposure could be in your imagination as well as in real life (for example, thinking

about going to these places where the accident took place, and actually going to visit the place).

Being stronger ensures you avoid getting overwhelmed by the pain recalling it. You'll have to confront the doubts for this to happen, and be prepared to think about the situation. You should not have to do any of this at once. You need to speak quickly at first and then gradually in-depth about what happened, and cope with the disturbing emotions, so you can just get on with your life. The goal is to face the fears as well as the terrible memories so they don't get in your life anymore.

3.2 How to Help Children Cope with Traumas

Like adults, the responses of the majority of children go away over time. Parents and family may help recuperate the child in several ways:

Keep talking – on what's going on, how family members sound about what each other want. It helps keep children from becoming lonely, depressed, and incomprehensive. Convince them that they are healthy, and now they're being cared for. Pay attention to the story, and speak to them. Honest, an accessible conversation is better for children because the unseen is sometimes more terrifying than the truth. Even the really young children know something is happening and, again, it's easier for any of them to face the reality than the unknown. Some kids need extra motivation or special care, particularly at bedtime. Allowing children to show how they felt. Feelings are part of the process of Recovery. Help the child to work through that and give them privacy. Enjoy something as a family, and ensure your time is spent together for enjoyable and satisfying moments. Shared laughter takes a family through a number of tough periods. Keep clear on family roles. Don't let your child bear too much obligation for too long, even if they want to take care of an upset parent. Equally important, after a trauma, is not to become too overprotective of your child. Seek to explain why they don't do anything for a bit, including going to school or supporting at home but think about how they'll get back to regular activity as quickly as they can.

Like older people, most children, with the love and support of their family and friends, will adapt and evolve through the crisis. However, whether the responses of the child are especially serious or repeated, or if you have any questions regarding how the child responds to a stressful incident, do not hesitate to call anyone qualified to assess the condition and guide you.

3.3 How to Cope with Crisis

Any shift as a by-product causes tension. However, incidents in our lives often become stressful enough to trigger a disaster, and the levels of tension become sometimes unmanageable. These emergencies involve being infected with a major health problem, coping with the effects of a natural catastrophe, or being adversely impacted by a human tragedy, while incidents with reduced magnitude may often constitute a crisis. There are any safe methods of coping with a situation and moving over to the other side.

Here are a few tips to bear in mind when addressing a situation.

Process Your Feelings

Whether you're writing in your journal, chatting to a close friend, or visiting a psychiatrist, it's crucial to bring words into the perspective to help express it. When you work through the situation, for fear that you may 'wallow' too long and get 'stuck,' you might be inclined to suppress your feelings however expressing your feelings would help you to step past them then let them go.

Lessen Your Stress Response

If you are having a crisis (even when someone around you is having a crisis), the stress reaction of your body will get activated and remain activated, leaving you in a state of continuous tension. Although becoming "relaxed" in the middle or during a crisis can be tough, you should practice stress reduction strategies that will decrease the severity of your stress rates, allow you to counteract the stress reaction, and become more comfortable in the face of what is next.

Focus on What's Important

It's necessary to concentrate the time on coping with the consequences of a crisis. Only going through the day is an achievement, and it will be important to paring out the obligations to achieve just that. Order take-out so that you can cut back on shopping and eating, place unwanted obligations on pause, and instead concentrate on what actually needs to be accomplished and maintain your physical and mental strength healthy.

Find Support

While people are conscious of the pain, they're apt to give help; now's the time to take that on. Let your loved ones make your burden easier by assisting with chores or by providing a sympathetic ear. If you're up to it you will return the favor later because they require more. By having assistance, you will feel happier, so people would also feel stronger by being willing to do more to help. That's what best friends do.

Be Patient

Many people who live with a tragedy or depression question whether their adverse responses are a reflection of vulnerability, or whether they are doing it the 'right' way. Although there are healthier ways to deal with stressful circumstances, be careful with your emotions and responses to issues. It's normal to feel after a big – or even mild – trauma 'not yourself,' so acknowledging yourself so your emotions can help you feel stronger and make it easier to handle.

Take Care of Yourself

Make sure to follow a balanced diet, get adequate sleep, workout frequently, and do other stuff to keep the body working at its highest, to stop contributing to the issues. Often, consider doing stuff you usually like, such as watching a video, reading a nice novel, or planting to ease any of the tension you're going through.

Seek Help When Needed

When you have recurrent thoughts and emotions, have persistent dreams or are unable to go about your life the way you should because of your response to the incident, particularly after many weeks, you might want to speak to a doctor about the condition and make sure you have the help you should. Also, though you don't have some big issues, just believe like talking to somebody may be a smart idea, it's best to be on the side of having some support. It's a cool and smart way to look after yourself.

Chapter 4. Dialectical Behavioral Therapy to Relieve Borderline Personality Disorder

A borderline personality disorder is a syndrome characterized by a persistent cycle of changing moods, behavior, and self-image. Such signs also give rise to impulsive behavior and relationship issues. Someone with a borderline personality disorder may suffer severe episodes of rage, anxiety, and depression that may last from a few days to weeks. People with a borderline personality disorder can experience mood changes and display confusion about their view of themselves and their position in the world. As a consequence, their priorities and values could rapidly shift. People with an unstable personality disorder often appear to have strong interpretations of issues like all positive or all evil. Other people's opinions can also swiftly change. A person who is treated one day as a friend can be viewed as an adversary or a liar the next. These shifting sensations can result in intense, dysfunctional relationships.

Other signs or symptoms may include:

- Efforts to prevent actual or potential abandonment, such as rapid initiation of romantic (physical or emotional) relations or cessation in contact with others in expectation in abandonment

- A frequent yet dysfunctional pattern of relationships with families, acquaintances yet loved ones, sometimes moving from deep closeness and affection (idealization) to severe hate or rage (devaluation)

- Distorted and dysfunctional self-image or self-absorption

- Impulsive and sometimes risky habits such as gambling, unhealthy sex, misuse of drugs, careless driving, and consuming binge. If these behaviors happen primarily throughout a period of high mood or power, they may well be signs of depressive disorder and not a borderline personality disorder

- Self-harming actions, including cuts
- Recurring suicidal feelings or attacks
- Intense and extremely unpredictable moods, every episode ranging from a few hours to many days
- Chronic Emptiness Feelings
- Inappropriate, extreme rage, or temper management issues
- Trusting problems which are often caused by unreasonable distrust of the motives of others

- Feelings of dissociation, including such a feeling of being separated from oneself, seeing oneself from outside one 's body or feeling unreal

A certified mental health expert such as a psychologist, psychiatrist, or a clinical social worker that is experienced in the diagnosis and treatment of mental illnesses can make a diagnosis regarding borderline personality disorder by completing an in-depth interview, including debate of symptoms, conducting a comprehensive and detailed medical examination that can assist rule out other conditions and causes of symptoms and inquire about them.

Many psychiatric disorders also cause borderline personality disorder. Co-occurring conditions can make it more difficult to identify and manage borderline personality disorder, particularly if signs of other illnesses correlate with borderline personality disorder signs. For instance, an individual with borderline personality disorder could also be more likely to encounter depression symptoms, bipolar or anxiety disorders, eating disorders, or substance use disorders. Historically, borderline personality disorder has been deemed hard to treat. But with new and innovative, evidence-based treatment, numerous people with this disorder experience fewer severe symptoms, and improvement in the quality of life. It is essential that individuals with borderline personality disorder seek advanced, evidence-based care by a properly qualified physician. The individual cannot profit from certain forms of care, including therapy given by a doctor or therapist who is not properly qualified. Some variables influence the amount of time it takes for symptoms to change after therapy begins, and individuals with borderline personality disorder and their family ones need to stay vigilant and have appropriate care through recovery.

Dialectical behavioral counseling is a standardized clinical program focused on cognitive-behavioral concepts founded by Dr. Marsha Linehan in the early 1990s for the diagnosis of borderline personality disorder (BPD) parasuicidal behavior in women. A borderline personality disorder is a psychiatric condition that involves signs such as frenzied attempts to prevent real or perceived rejection, dysfunctional marriages, identity disruption, impulsive and threatening behavior, frequent suicidal or self-mutilation behavior, affective dysfunction, feelings of depression, anger-control problems and/or stress-related delusional thinking or dissociation. BPD's lifetime prevalence is about 6 percent. Borderline personality disorder represents considerably higher health care costs compared with both major depressive disorder as well as other personality disorders. Such increased care rates can be due to a larger level of hospitalizations, more regular trips to emergency departments, and wider usage of ambulance services.

The term "dialectical" refers to the interaction of opposing ideas. "Dialectical" refers, within Dialectical Behavior Therapy, to the unification of both affirmation and change as basic needs to improve. Dialectical behavioral treatment helps to treat the effects of Borderline Personality Disorder by combining maladaptive habits with healthy coping strategies such as understanding, cognitive effectiveness, control of impulses, and acceptance to pain. Evidence has since demonstrated that medication is effective in addressing conditions of alcohol use, mood disturbances, posttraumatic stress disorder, and eating disorders in both adults and youth. Given the frequently-comorbid clinical effects of bipolar personality disorder in individuals taking part in dialectical behavioral treatment, psychopharmacological treatments are also deemed sufficient adjunctive care. The chapter aims at explaining the therapy's fundamental concepts as well as focusing on the role of pharmacotherapy as an adjunctive medication for Borderline personality disorder symptoms. Numerous randomized clinical experiments have been performed to assess the efficacy of Dialectical behavioral treatment in Borderline personality disorder. Since 1991 the Linehan Institute has published a collection of RCTs that evaluate research on dialectical behavioral therapy. This summary shows that dialectical behavior therapy has been much more effective in various places than community-based treatment-as-usual, which include reducing parasuicidal behavior patterns, continuing to increase medication compliance, and limiting the number of hospital admissions.

Comorbid substance use and abuse, binge eating disorder, anxiety or depression, and bulimia nervosa have also been effective in dialectical behavior therapy. Additionally, key diagnosis of trichotillomania, depressive illness, eating disorders, attention deficit hyperactivity disorder, (e.g., binge eating, bulimia nervosa, anorexia nervosa), mental disturbance youth, and Posttraumatic disorder have been reported. It is noticeable that many of the aforementioned psychological conditions share clinical criteria with Borderline personality disorder, such as impulsiveness, labile mood, personality problems, suicidal behaviors, and/or risky behavior. Such mutual goal signs potentially lead to the efficacy of dialectic behavioral treatment through illnesses.

Research Support

DBT was the very first psychotherapy found to be successful in the diagnosis of BPD, the most comprehensive method of psychiatric study, in randomized clinical studies. DBT is known as the first-line "gold standard" therapy for borderline personality disorder. While DBT is not the only therapy now that has demonstrated efficacy in a controlled trial, it has gone up significantly evidence base and is probably one of the greatest BPD treatments in terms of recorded success rates. Evidence shows that DBT decreases clinical hospitalization, drug usage, and suicidal activity successfully. There were also substantial decreases in hospital visits, self-injurious habits, and the frequency of unstable symptoms among the research participants.

Theory

Dialectical behavioral treatment is focused on Dr. Linehan's hypothesis that the central issue with Borderline personality disorder is an emotional dysregulation arising from combining genes, both hereditary and other biological risk factors, and an emotionally dysfunctional developmental atmosphere where parents, for example, threaten, trivialize or react erratically to the child's emotional speech.

DBT's emphasis is on having the individual develop and implement techniques that can reduce the dysregulation of feelings and ineffective efforts to deal with intense emotions.

There are 4 types of skills (main) that DBT covers in skills training. These are:

1. Mindfulness Meditation Skills

Meditation mindfulness skills focus on being fully present in the current situation. Such abilities rely on understanding how to recognize, interpret, and engage in all interactions, including feelings, perceptions, reactions, and events that happen directly in the world, without defining such interactions as "positive" or "evil." They are called key abilities that are required to effectively incorporate certain DBT techniques.

For instance, individuals with BPD can find themselves overcome with emotions during a dispute and then act on those feelings without considering the implications. Mindfulness abilities help us understand how certain feelings should be perceived and controlled, helping them to stand back and react more effectively.

2. Interpersonal Effectiveness Skills

This ability training focuses on learning how to effectively express your desires and resolve partnership disputes.

3. Distress Tolerance Skills

The pain management training program encourages finding strategies to embrace and manage anxiety without doing somet hing that, for example, would cause discomfort or self-harm in the long run.

If faced with intense emotions, a person with BPD can indulge in impulsive or dangerous behaviors to escape from what feels like an overwhelming sensation. Substance usage, abuse, inappropriate consumption of alcohol, and other dangerous acts are only a few examples of activities that one may indulge in to feel comfortable momentarily. The problem is that in the long term, those behaviors make things worse. Distress management skills help individuals to know how to properly deal with these feelings and react more proactively.

4. Emotion Regulation Skills

Patients learn to recognize and control emotional responses in this module. Regulating feelings include increasing or minimizing feelings so that they can respond appropriately and accomplish individual objectives. Gaining these interpersonal skills helps individuals with BPD to understand their feelings correctly and discover opportunities to control and communicate them in positive, non-destructive opportunities. Examples of a person's skills may involve understanding how to recognize feelings, modifying habits to improve the circumstance, or discovering strategies to manage the anger without lashing out.

Effectiveness

DBT is not a solution for borderline personality disorders but can be very successful in reducing or trying to manage the condition 's symptoms. One study found that after a year of recovery for dialectical behavior counseling 77 percent of the people no longer met the BPD criterion.

Getting Help

Whether you are involved in understanding more about DBT, the Behavioral Tech platform provides a range of services. To read more about DBT and Dr. Linehan's principles, you can always check online. It can help you find the resources for DBT that are available in your area. Additionally, you may seek a referral from a psychiatrist, psychologist, or some other behavioral health provider to someone who is trained in DBT.

4.1 The Difference Between DBT and Didactic Therapy

Didactic counseling is a community intervention that is most commonly used by people with drug use problems to show them the truth to inform them, whereas DBT is usually used in borderline personality disorder treatment.

Conclusion

Motivational interviewing is a therapy approach that includes improving the desire of an individual to improve by four guiding concepts, defined by the acronym RULE: suppressing the righting reflex; recognizing the patient's motivations; listening empathically; and encouraging the patient.

This kind of therapy is used to encourage the patients suffering from certain delusions like they are not enough for something or not good enough for someone. The basic and main aim of the therapist is to encourage and appreciate their patients on everything and their efforts. The main point of Motivational Interviewing is to bring out all the negative thoughts in a person's mind and fill it with positive thoughts. To make the patient love themselves no matter what. A person in need of Motivational Interviewing is suffering from insecurities and complexities. A therapist has to make their patients believe that their insecurities are baseless and they can do better than that they are better than they think they are. It is important for everyone. Self-love is the first stage for anything otherwise, a person can do nothing in his/her life.

This book is a complete guide on what Motivational Interviewing is. How it can help you to cope with certain issues. Besides that, auto-counseling is also a thing that can be helpful for specific persons to overcome any trauma or a crisis that they are going through. All of us need to deal with our traumas and emotional disturbances if we want to move on in life. Otherwise, we are simply good for nothing if we cannot cope with ourselves. Traumas and emotional disorders can lead to self-hate and that is the biggest obstacle in anyone's life. It hinders your success as well.

CPSIA information can be obtained
at www.ICGtesting.com
Printed in the USA
BVHW051509080321
601999BV00001BB/34